· LITTLE-KNOWN FACTS ·

ANIMALS

Diarmuid Ó Catháin

It's a little-known fact,

you may not have read...

A shrimp's heart
is found in its head!

It's a little-known fact, you're unlikely to hear...

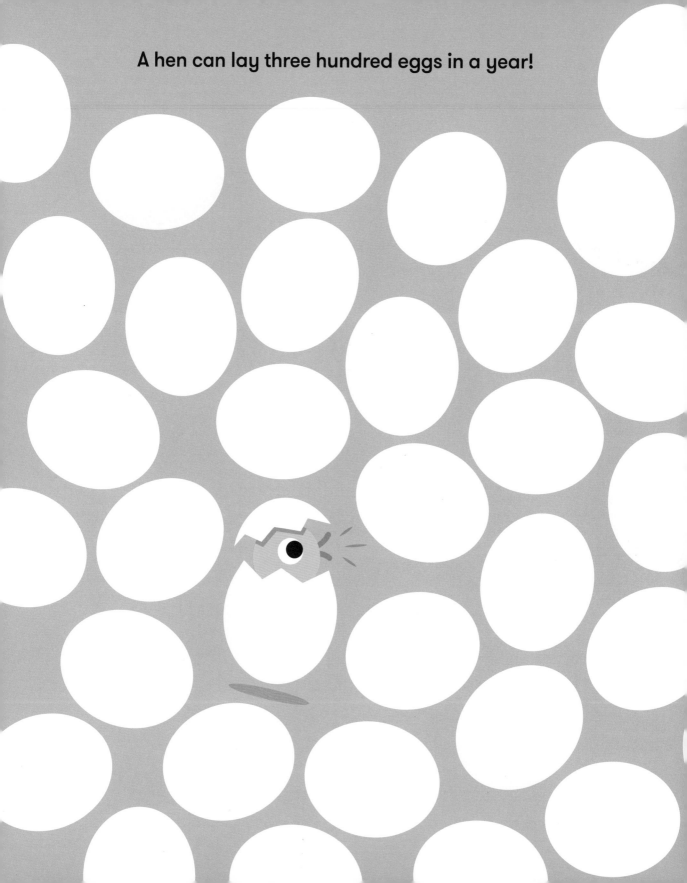

A hen can lay three hundred eggs in a year!

It's a little-known fact, you won't soon forget...

A pelican uses its beak as a net!

It's a little-known fact, and what a surprise...

A snake can eat things many times its own size!

It's a little-known fact, and studies do show...

A beaver's teeth continue to grow!

It's a little-known fact,

that far from tone deaf...

Houseflies hum in the key of F!
Bzzzzzzzz!

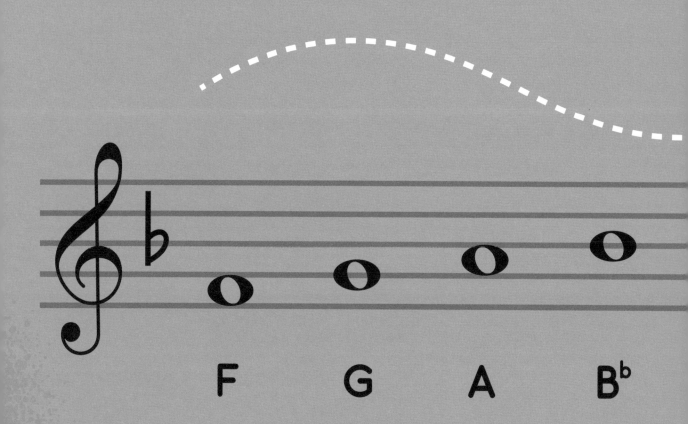

C D E F

It's a little-known fact, and listen up dear...

A giraffe is able to lick its own ear!

It's a little-known fact,

that once it has chewed...

A sloth can take two weeks to digest its food!

It's a little-known fact,
that unlike a boat...

A hippopotamus is unable to float!

It's a little-known fact, and here's the scoop...

Wombats make
square-shaped poop!

It's a little-known fact, that may come as a fright...

A bat eats thousands of insects a night!

It's a little-known fact,
and just happens to rhyme...

Some snails can sleep for three years at a time!

It's a little-known fact, that when ready to eat...

A butterfly tastes its food with its feet!

It's a little-known fact,
shhhh don't tell anyone...

Some species of turtle
breathe through their bum!

It's a little-known fact, and cause for applause...

Moray eels have two sets of jaws!

Nyom nyom!

It's a little-known fact, and may sound insane...

An ostrich's eye is bigger than its brain!

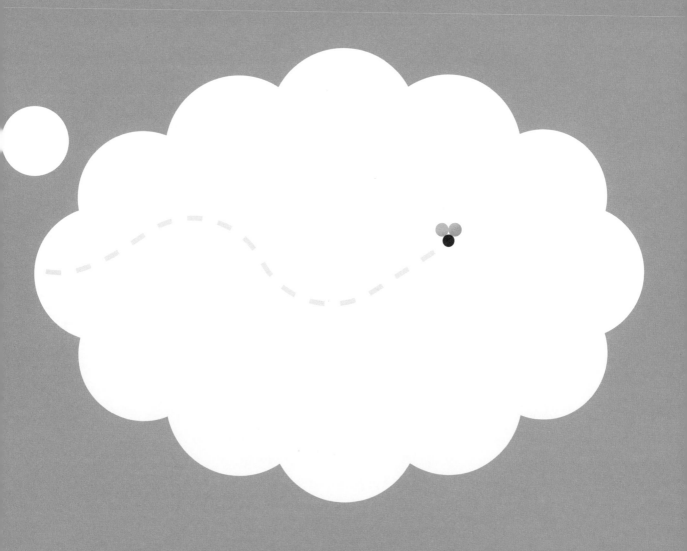

It's a little-known fact,

which may cause a fuss...

A colossal squid is bigger than a bus!

And it's a little-known fact,
that inside your head...

Are hundreds of facts
   you could tell me instead!